START-A-CRAFT

Woodcarving

Get started in a new craft with easy-to-follow
projects for beginners

PETER BERRY

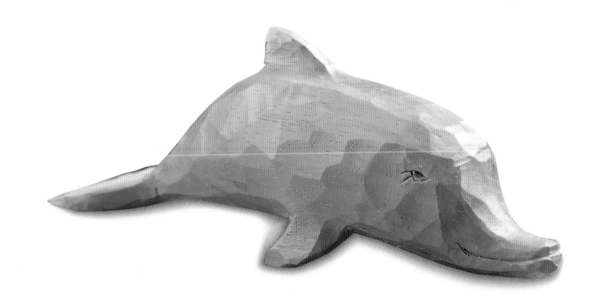

CHARTWELL
BOOKS, INC.

A QUINTET BOOK

Published by Chartwell Books
A Division of Book Sales, Inc.
114 Northfield Avenue
Edison, New Jersey 08837

ISBN 0-7858-0612-1

This book was designed and produced by
Quintet Publishing Limited
6 Blundell Street
London N7 9BH

Creative Director: Richard Dewing
Designer: James Lawrence
Project Editor: Diana Steedman
Editor: Gail Dixon-Smith
Photographer: Keith Waterton

Typeset in Great Britain by
Central Southern Typesetters, Eastbourne
Manufactured in Singapore by Eray Scan Pte Ltd
Printed in China by Leefung-Asco Printers Ltd

DEDICATION

**This book is dedicated to my wife Lynn for all her
support and to my son David and daughter Sara.**

ACKNOWLEDGMENTS

Thanks are due to Ashley Iles (Edge Tools) Ltd
for supply of equipment,
John Boddy (Fine Wood and Tool Store)
for supply of materials and Trudy Hills for help
in preparing the text.

CONTENTS

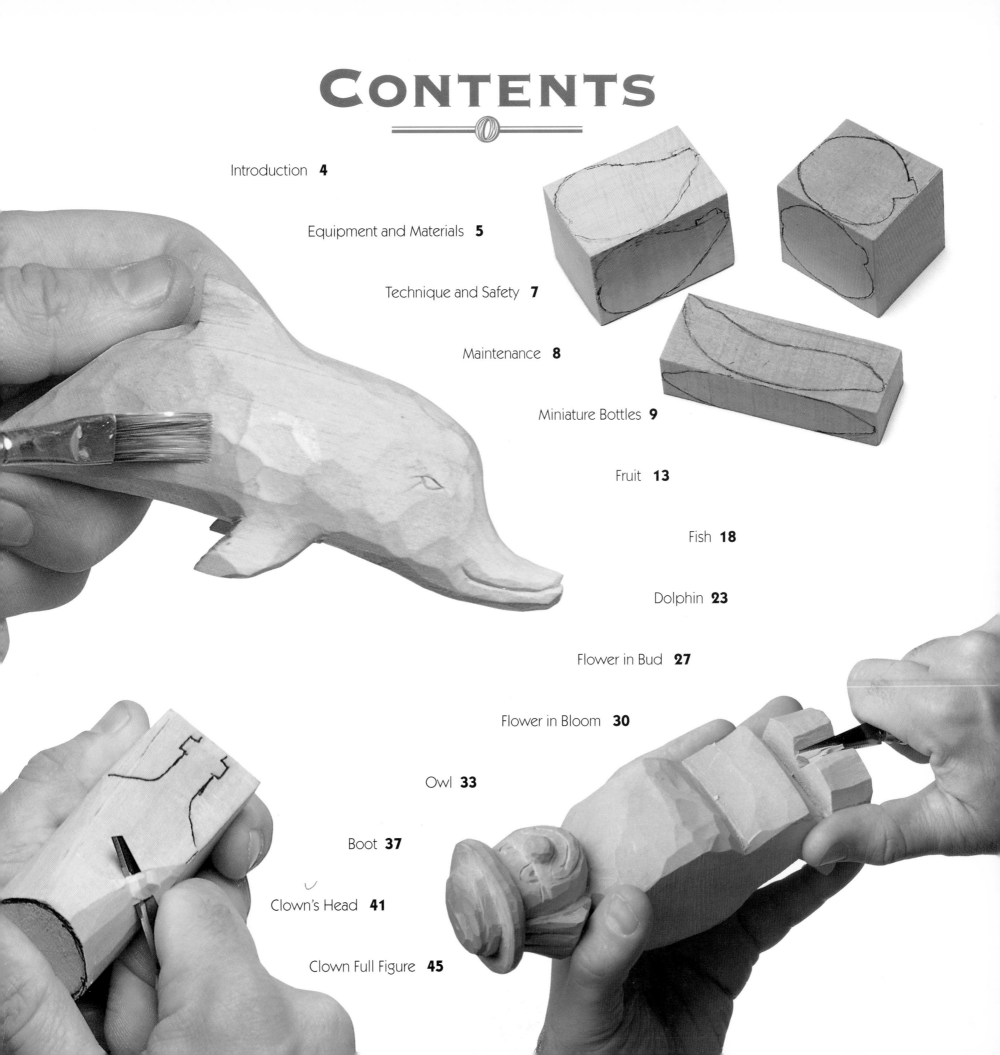

INTRODUCTION

Carving, whatever the material, is one of the most basic forms of art. Carving wood, a natural and most attractive resource, has held a fascination for mankind since the beginning of time. We often see wonderful examples of this craft, which might lead us to assume that it is not for us. However, reality is quite the reverse – a sharp knife, a piece of wood, some varnish or paints, a desire to learn, and a little imagination are all that are required to embark upon a craft which will give you countless hours of pleasure and amaze your friends. All the projects in this book have been designed so that they can be achieved with no previous experience. The plans are drawn to scale so they can be copied or traced to use as simple templates. Each step is clearly illustrated and carefully explained. The finished carving can be either varnished or painted and clear illustration and instruction is given on both of these techniques. The projects have been designed to quickly increase your skill and confidence as you work your way through the book. All you need to bring is enthusiasm and a desire to learn – so let's go!

EQUIPMENT AND MATERIALS

TOOLS

Would-be carvers are often put off by the thought of having to purchase and maintain a large variety of woodcarvers' chisels and accessories. However, the projects in this book have been designed to enable you to complete them by simply using a knife. There are many knives on the market which can be used for carving.

STAINLESS STEEL CRAFT KNIFE SET

This is the simplest to use and probably the least expensive to buy. The blades are interchangeable and should be replaced when they become blunt.

STEEL CRAFT KNIFE SET

This is similar to the set just described but the blades can be sharpened. The basic techniques of sharpening are described later.

FOLDING OR FIXED BLADE KNIVES

These knives can be either purpose-made fixed blade knives or the simple folding penknife. Both these types can be sharpened.

CHISELS

While the carvings in this book can be completed simply with a set of knives they can of course be produced by using carving chisels. A basic set would comprise of ¾ inch shallow gouge, a ⅜ inch shallow gouge and a ¼ inch "V" tool.

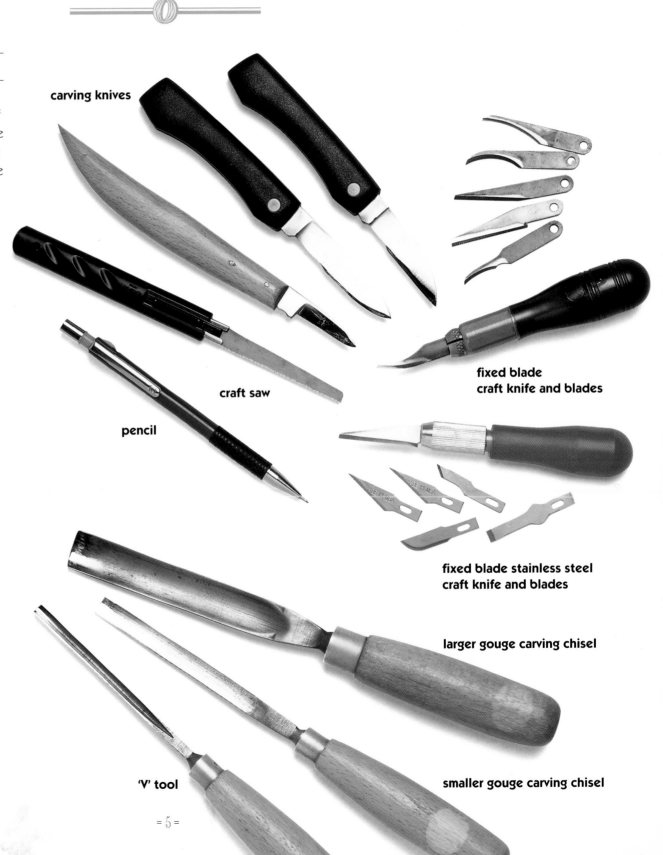

carving knives

fixed blade craft knife and blades

craft saw

pencil

fixed blade stainless steel craft knife and blades

larger gouge carving chisel

'V' tool

smaller gouge carving chisel

WOOD

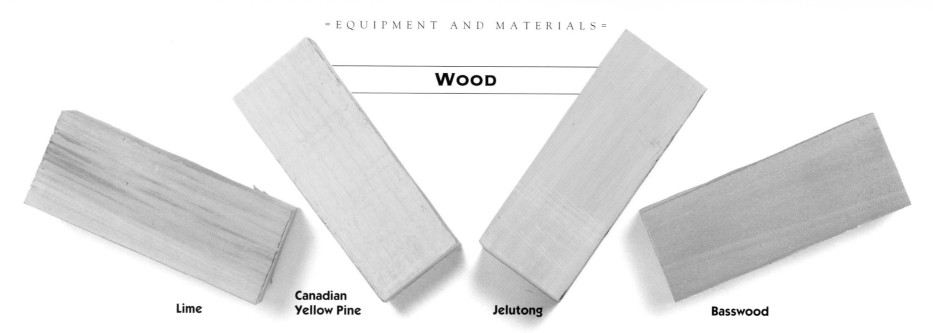

Lime

Canadian Yellow Pine

Jelutong

Basswood

There is a bewildering number of timbers in the world all having their unique properties of texture and color. In practice some will be more suitable for carving than others. An ideal wood for our projects would be straight grained, not too dense and light in color. Examples are, English Lime, American Basswood, Canadian Yellow Pine, and Malaysian Jelutong all of which I have used to good effect. Good craft outlets should be able to assist you in obtaining the right wood and there are many published magazines on woodwork generally to point you in the right direction.

However, since the projects are quite small and do not require enormous amounts of wood to be removed, you may find that experimenting with that bit of scrap wood you were about to throw away also works quite well.

PAINTS AND BRUSHES

Acrylic paint works very well on light wood and a small basic set of colors and two or three brushes is all you need.

VARNISHES

Many wood varnishes are sold and I would recommend acrylic, water-based varnish. It can be used on the bare wood directly or as a finishing coat to a painted carving. Acrylic varnish is easy to apply with a brush and I suggest a satin finish rather than a high gloss.

TECHNIQUE AND SAFETY

Cutting away from yourself with the grain.

Cutting toward yourself with the grain.

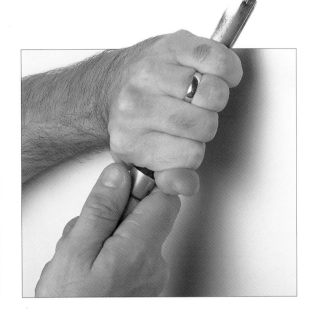

Using the chisel for heavy work.

Using the chisel for light work.

Cutting across the grain.

Cutting into the grain will split the wood.

Since knife-carving involves holding both the knife (which must be sharp at all times) and the wood in your hands, it is essential that due regard is given to employing safe and effective cutting techniques.

It is important to ensure that wherever possible you keep your hands away from the line of the blade whether you are cutting away from or toward yourself.

Your thumbs play a very important part in knife-carving as they provide both power and control at the same time.

When using a chisel it is important to have both hands on the chisel at all times.

A further point to note when carving wood is to try to understand how the grain runs. Wood grain can be likened to thousands of tiny straws

compacted together. You can safely cut with them and even across them but you cannot cut directly into them without splitting.

TIP
• It is a good idea to have a first-aid kit handy when working with sharp tools.

MAINTENANCE

Whatever craft you embark upon, looking after your equipment is essential whether it be keeping your pencils sharp or your brushes clean and dry. Keeping your cutting edges sharp is an essential part of woodcarving.

If you are using pre-sharpened stainless steel craft knives do not continue using the blades when they are blunt, throw them away and insert new ones.

If your knife is not the pre-sharpened type, you will need to obtain a good edge on it and keep it that way.

Sharpening a knife is a fairly simple process. You require an oilstone to get the blade to the right shape and a leather strop to create a smooth razor-edge finish. The strop can be made from a piece of leather or old belt and an oilstone can be obtained from most good hardware stores.

The oilstone needs to be held firmly in place, a smearing of lubricating oil applied and the blade drawn across the stone several times on each side. The blade should be held almost flat and the process repeated until the metal becomes rather ragged along its full length. This burr (or rough edge) can be felt carefully with the finger or thumb.

The next step is to repeat the process on the leather strop after it has been smeared with any metal-polishing agent. Tubes of polishing paste can be found in most hardware or car accessory stores and work very well. Stropping the blade from side to side is continued until the burr is smooth and the blade is sharp. Clean it with a cloth or paper towel if necessary.

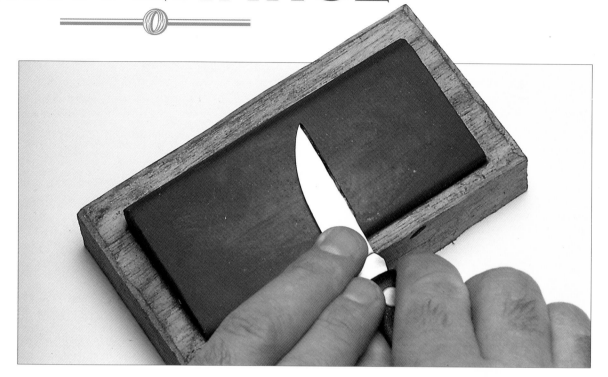

Using the oilstone to sharpen a blade.

Using the leather strop to get a razor-edge.
Sharpening chisels follows the same basic principles but because of the variety of shapes the process is more involved. I would recommend reference to more specialized books for information on chisel sharpening.

MINIATURE BOTTLES

The first thing I ever carved was a miniature bottle. If you keep the lines fairly straight it is quite an effective subject and provides you with a good introduction to some simple techniques. Bottles come in an enormous variety of shapes and sizes.

You will need

◊ Block of wood 1⅛ x 1⅛ x 3½ inches
◊ Knife
◊ Varnish or paint to finish

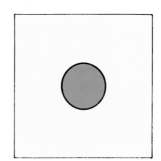

TIP
• To help draw the circles at either end, mark lines diagonally from corner to corner, then mark lines horizontally and perpendicular.

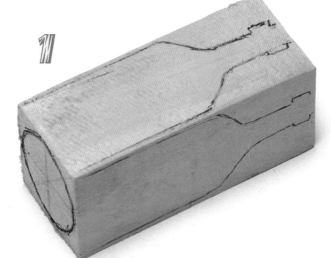

1 Trace around one of the plans to create a template then transfer the outline to your block of wood. Draw the end shapes of the bottle on the top and bottom of the block.

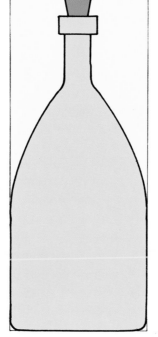

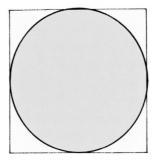

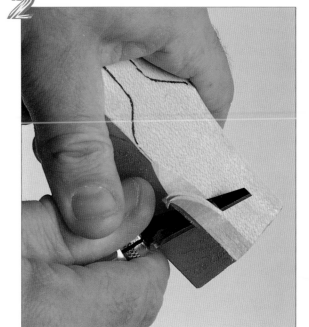

2 Start shaping around the base. You can carve away from or toward yourself, whichever feels more comfortable.

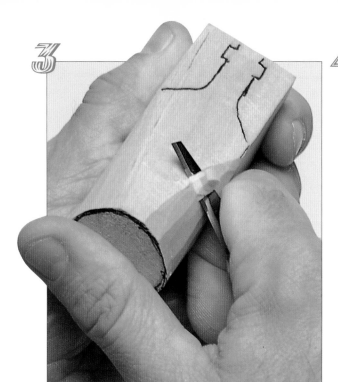

3 Complete the bottom of the bottle.

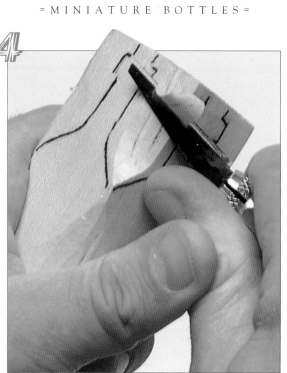

4 Start shaping the neck and shoulders.

5 Use your template to re-mark the neck and shoulders where the original marks have been carved away.

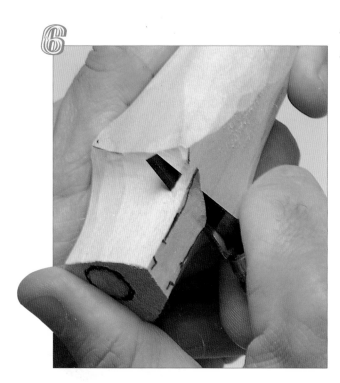

6 Continue to carve the neck to completion.

7 Compare your progress with the template.

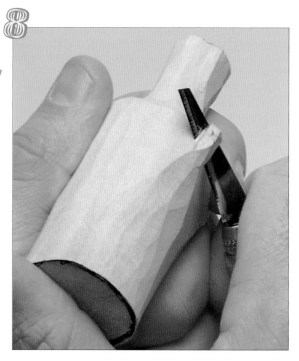

8 Complete the shaping of the shoulders.

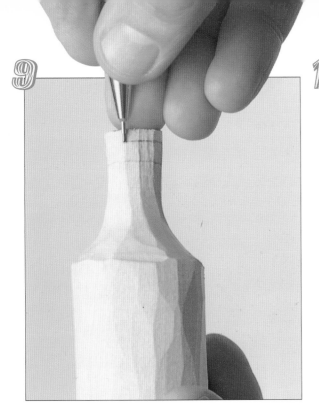

9 Refer to your plan and mark in the lip around the top of the neck.

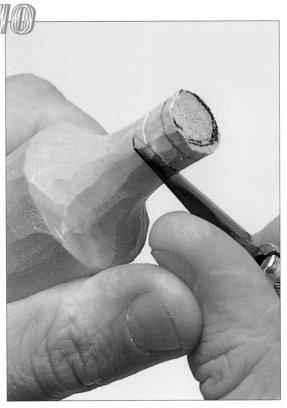

10 Score in the bottom part of the lip. To score, hold your knife firm and roll the bottle around the blade.

11 Carefully remove the wood from below the scored line.

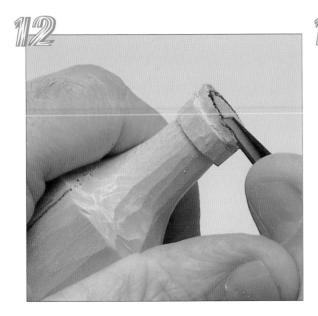

12 Do the same on the top line of the lip.

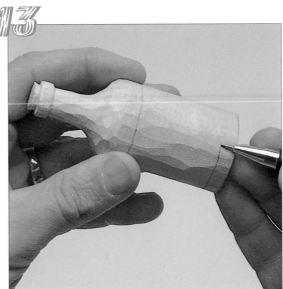

13 Add a little more interest by carving in a label – mark with your pencil.

14 Carve down to the scored line.

15

16

15 Carve wood away from around the label.

16 Varnish or paint to finish.

FRUIT

Carving fruit, with its variety of shapes, is a good progression from the miniature bottles. The rounded curves are a little more demanding than the bottles but they give you a further insight into dealing with grain. You can add some leaves to the basic shape to create a more interesting piece and add a little realism.

You will need
◊ Wood for the pear 2 x 2 x 3 inches
◊ Wood for the apple 2 x 2 x 2¼ inches
◊ Wood for the banana 1¼ x 1¼ x 4½ inches
◊ Knife
◊ Varnish or paints to finish

PEAR

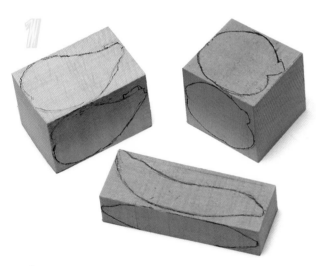

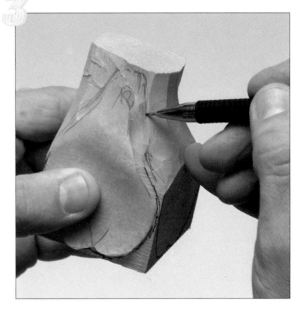

1 Start by creating templates from the plans and transferring the outline to your block of wood.

2 Start carving the pear toward the top end.

3 Continue the shaping using your template to guide you along. Re-mark the outline as you go to maintain a guide.

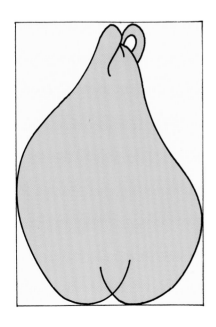

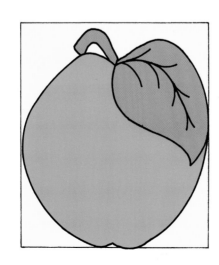

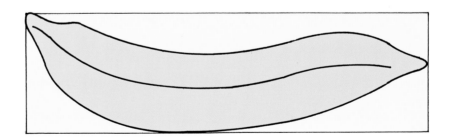

4 This stage is completed when the required shape of the top of the pear is achieved.

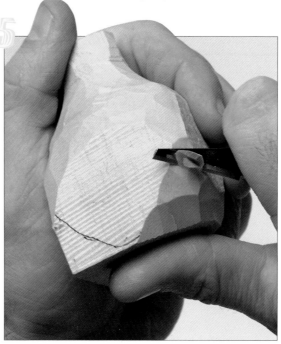

5 Once you are happy with the top, start shaping the bottom.

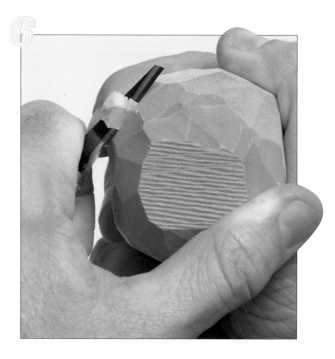

6 Continue shaping the base checking frequently from all angles.

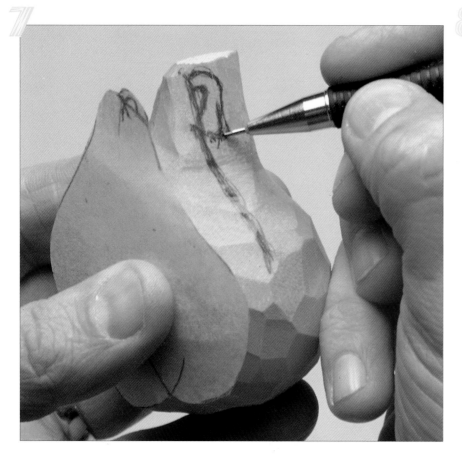

7 Look at your template and use it to mark the short stem on the top of the pear.

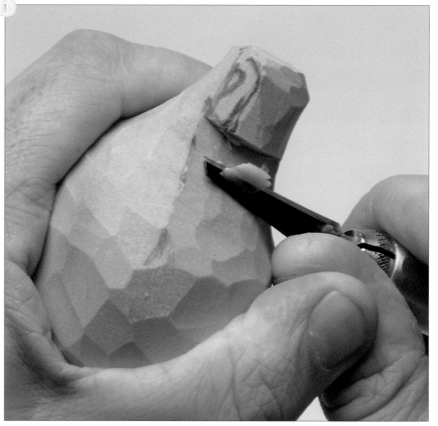

8 Carve around the shape taking care not to split away the wood.

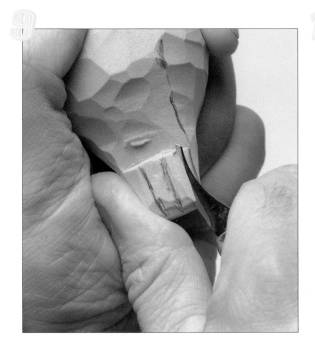

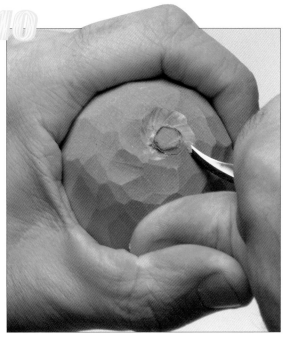

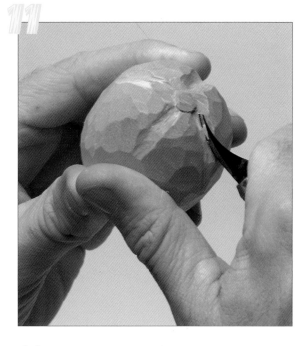

9 Carefully paring away the wood from either side of the stalk will complete this feature.

10 Add more detail by inserting the base end of the stalk. Simply score a small circle and carve the wood away from the outside.

11 Carve three or four shallow grooves into the base and the top to add a little more shape to the whole piece.

12 Paint or varnish to finish.

APPLE

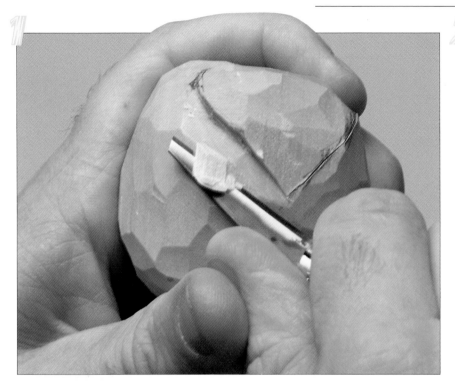

1 Refer to the early stages of carving the pear. Then mark the leaf on the basic shape of the apple, score the outline and start removing the wood from around the leaf.

2 Repeat the above process to create the stalk.

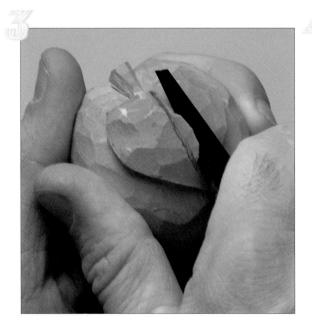

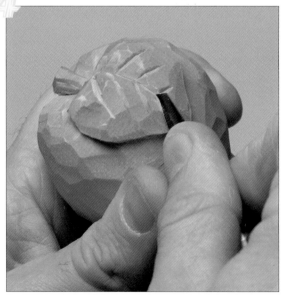

3 Add a little more detail to the leaf by cutting a narrow channel down the center.

4 Carve some narrow channels on either side of the center line to complete the carving. Paint or varnish to finish.

BANANA

1 The banana is a fairly straightforward shape but complements the apple and pear as a group. Refer to the plans and the stages of carving the pear for the basic approach.

2 Check your carving to ensure you have achieved a rough four-cornered end view, then paint or varnish to finish.

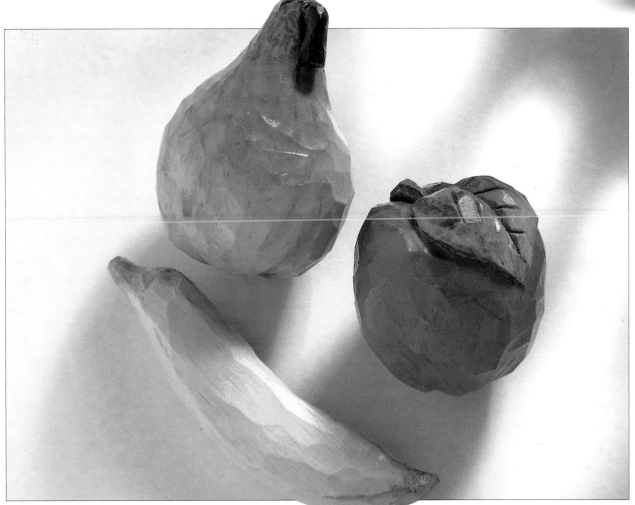

FISH

While the carvings in this book are ideally suited to using knives, I have used this project to describe the use of a basic set of chisels. Since chisels should be held in both hands, it will be necessary to hold your work tightly in a clamp or vice.

You will need
◊ Block of wood 5¼ x 3½ x 1 inch
◊ Piece of wood for backplate
  7¾ x 6 x ½ inches
◊ Set of 3 chisels
◊ Vice
◊ "G" clamp
◊ Screws or glue
◊ Varnish to finish

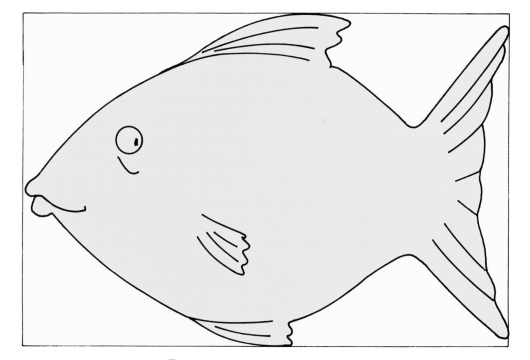

1 Transfer the plan to a piece of wood. You might find it helpful to put saw cuts in the wood to help remove the excess around the profile.

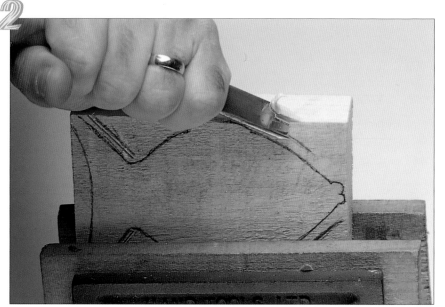

2 Clamp your work firmly in a vice and remove the wood around the head of the fish with your larger gouge as shown. You could use a saw cut to help you here.

3 Now, remove the wood from between the top fin and the tail. You may find it easier to use your smaller gouge here.

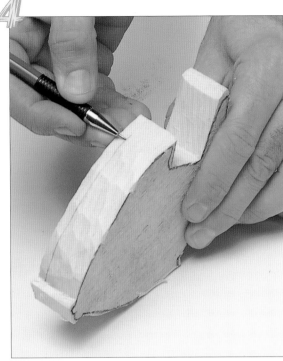

4 Having removed all the excess wood from around your plan, draw a line around the fish approximately ¼ inch in from the edge. Finish with a couple of coats of varnish.

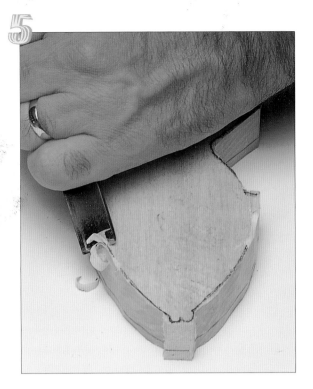

5 Use a "G" clamp to secure your carving to a firm surface and use your large gouge to slope the surface down to your marked line.

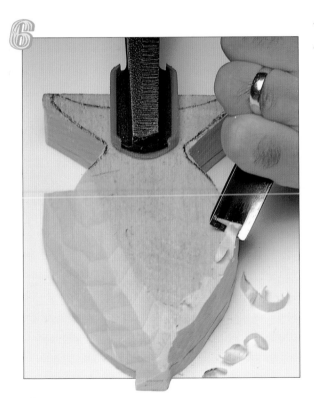

6 Continue the process of shaping the surface down to the marked edge.

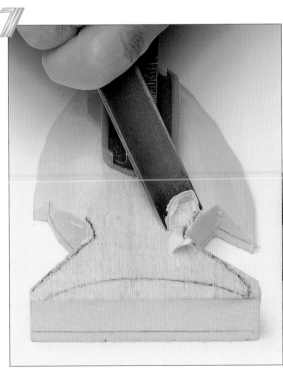

7 Take care with the shaping where the body meets the tail. You may need to carve across the grain to achieve a smooth cut.

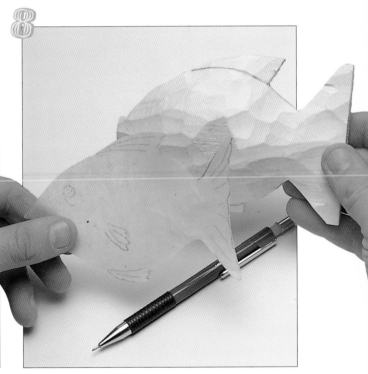

8 Refer to your plan and draw a line with your pencil to separate the two fins from the body.

9 Use your "V" tool chisel to carve a line along your pencil mark on the top fin.

10 Repeat the process on the lower fin.

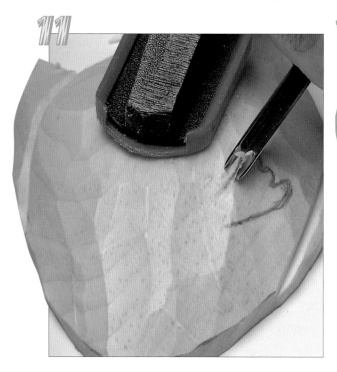

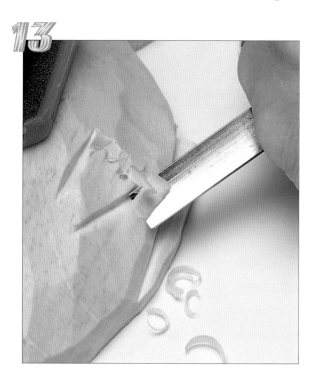

11 Having marked the fin on the body with your pencil, carve around the line with your "V" tool.

12 Take your small gouge and smooth out the sharp edges on your "V" tool cuts around the fins.

13 Remove the wood from around the "V" tool cuts forming the fin on the body.

14 Use your small gouge to remove wood from the tail to create a scallop edge.

15 Use your "V" tool to put some flowing lines on the fins and tail.

16 The fish has been carved on one side only, so you can choose a suitable size of timber to carve a backplate. I have used a piece of South American mahogany. After marking a line approximately ¾ inch around the border, use the large gouge to slope down the edge.

17 To complete the backplate carve over the surface lightly with the large gouge.

18 After screwing or gluing the two pieces together finish with a couple of coats of varnish.

DOLPHIN

Carving the dolphin is a natural progression from the fish. You could choose a wood with pronounced grain markings and sand the finished piece to create some smooth flowing lines. The dolphin is an elegant and attractive creature and your carving should try and capture these features.

You will need
◊ Block of wood 5½ x 2 x 1½ inches
◊ Knife
◊ Paint or varnish to finish

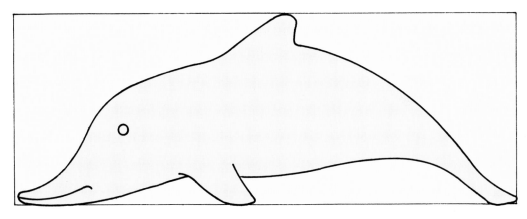

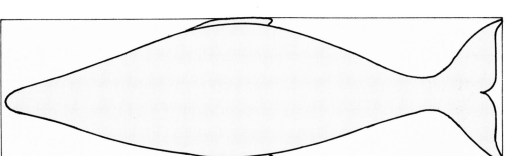

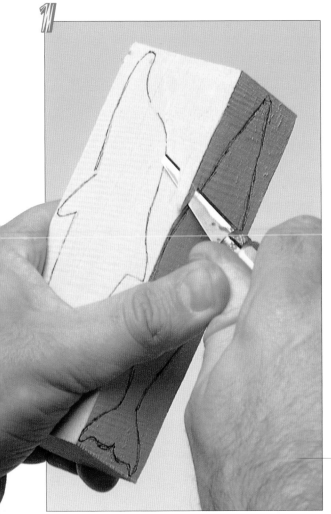

1 Transfer the plan to your block of wood. Although you will immediately carve away the top view, it is advisable to draw this in so you can get a good idea of how this looks.

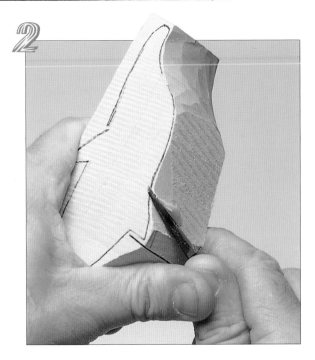

2 Carve away the wood from the top of the head to the top of the nose. You may like to try a saw cut to assist you here.

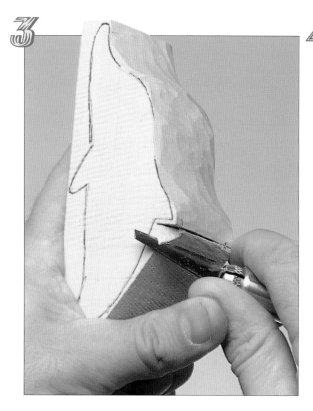

3 Having sawn down the back of the top fin, remove the wood behind the fin.

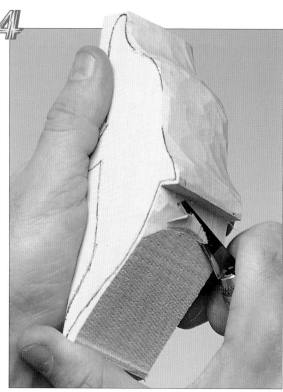

4 Continue to shape away behind the top fin using a saw cut to assist if you wish.

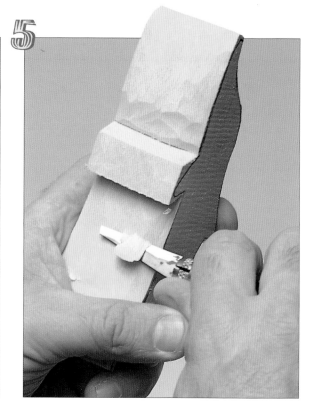

5 Repeat this process for the bottom fins, which you should treat as one for the time being.

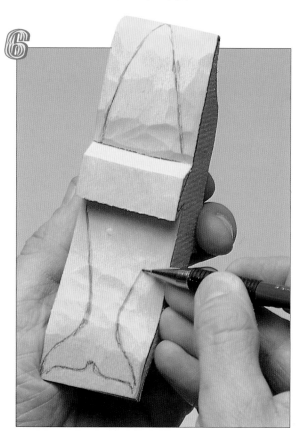

6 Referring to your plan, draw the shape of the dolphin on the bottom of your piece of wood.

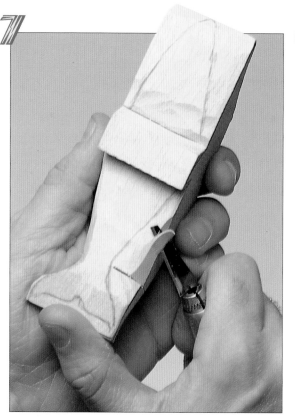

7 Use these guidelines to create the desired shape. A saw cut might help.

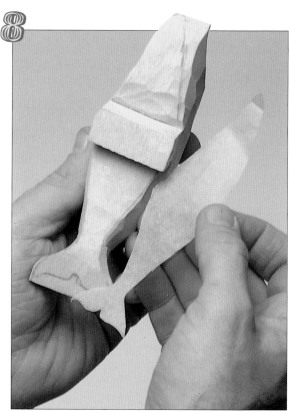

8 Compare your progress with the template.

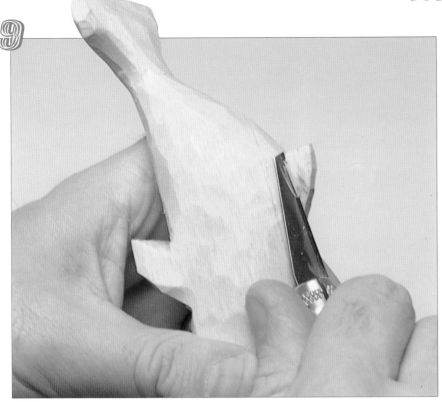

9 Round off the sharp corners on the whole of the body. You probably have a lot of wood to remove here so take your time and keep checking the overall shape.

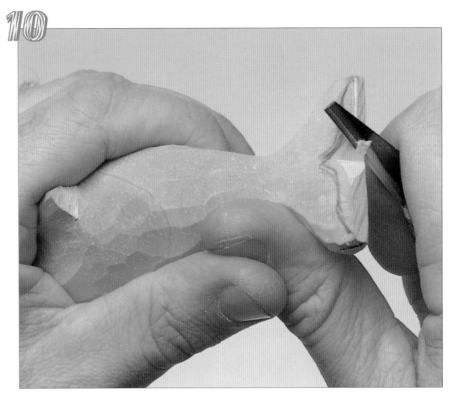

10 Look at your plan carefully and mark the end of the tail on the wood. Take care to create the desired shape.

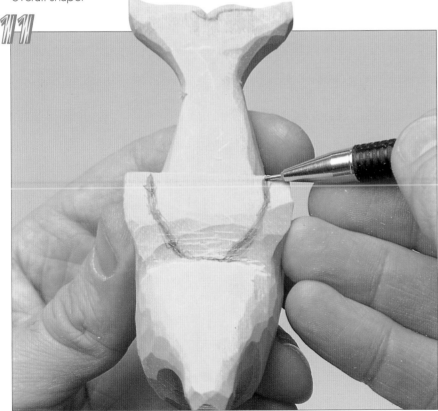

11 Mark two lines to separate the lower fins.

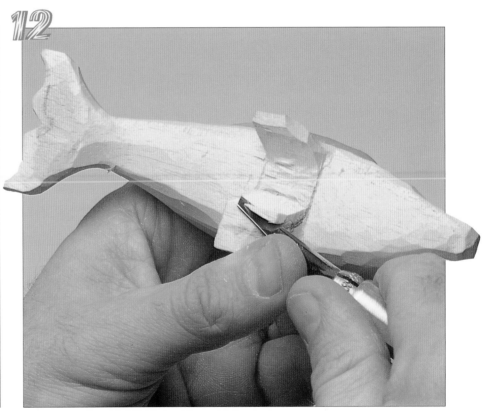

12 Carve away the wood between the two marked lines. You need to take care, particularly when the fins are approaching completion.

13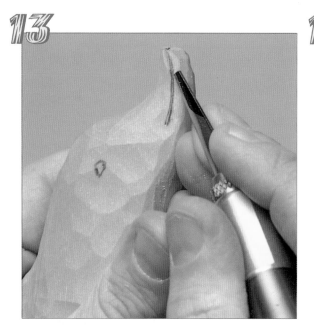

14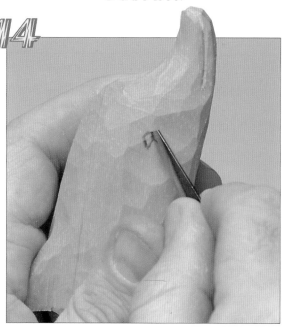

15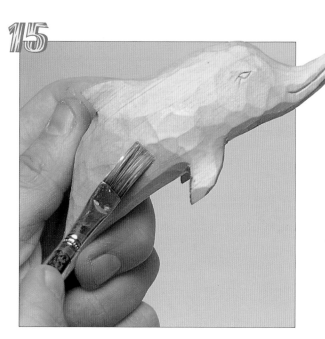

13 Mark in the mouth and eye with your pencil and lightly score the mouth with the tip of your knife. Open this cut slightly to create the mouth.

14 Lightly score the pencil mark forming the eye and carefully remove surrounding wood with the tip of your knife.

15 Paint or varnish to finish.

FLOWER IN BUD

Carving flowers is a rather unusual project. It requires the construction of the final piece from a number of smaller items. It is not really necessary to adhere rigidly to any known species rather leave it to your imagination. This is an opportunity to create some colorful and attractive items.

You will need
◊ Wood for the flower head 1½ x 1½ x 2¼ inches
◊ Wood for the stem ½ x ½ x 5 inches
◊ Wood for the leaf 2¼ x 1⅜ x ½ inch
◊ Knife
◊ Drill
◊ Glue
◊ Paint or varnish to complete

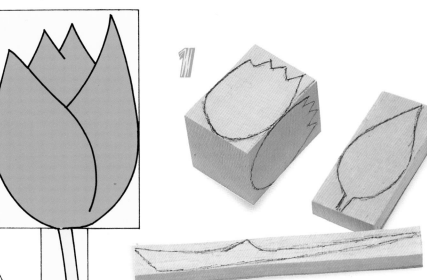

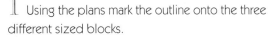

1 Using the plans mark the outline onto the three different sized blocks.

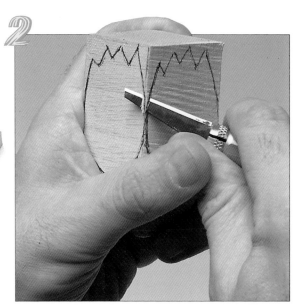

2 Start by carving the top half of the flower head.

3 Complete the top part of the flower head.

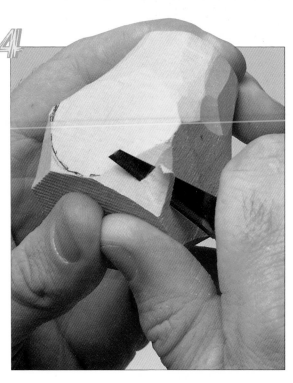

4 Start to work on the base of the flower head.

5 Once you have achieved the correct shape refer to the plan and mark the petals onto the flower.

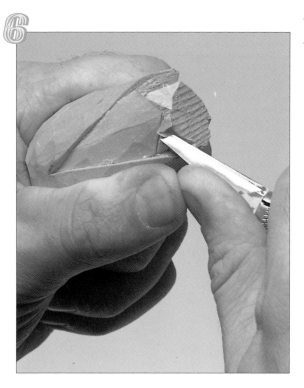

6 Score in the pencil marks and remove the wood from in-between to create the petals.

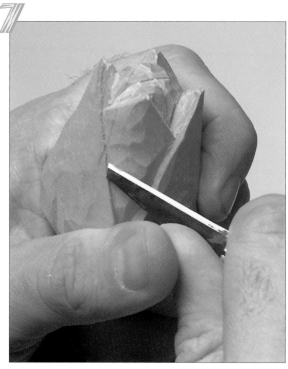

7 Continue shaping the petals referring to the plan to see how the top of the flower head is formed.

8 Take the block marked with the leaf and carve the general shape required.

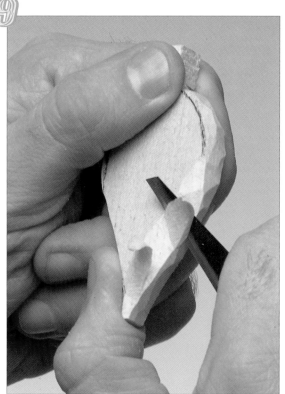

9 Work on the general shape of the leaf taking care to leave a piece at the base to be inserted in the stem.

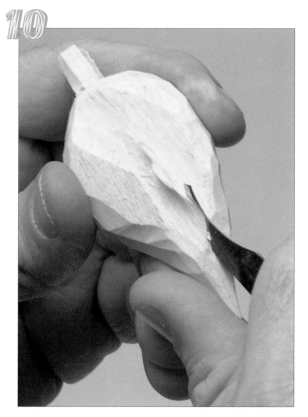

10 The final process is to carve the edges to produce a smooth rounded edge.

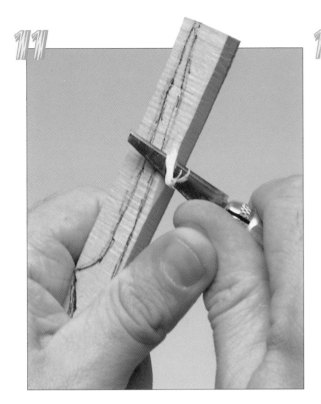

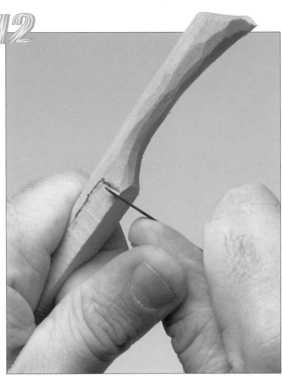

11 Take the stem and start rounding the shape generally.

12 Look at the plan to see how to carve the small platform to take the leaf.

13 The stem needs a small hole to take the leaf and it is advisable to hold the leaf against the stem to get an idea of the angle required.

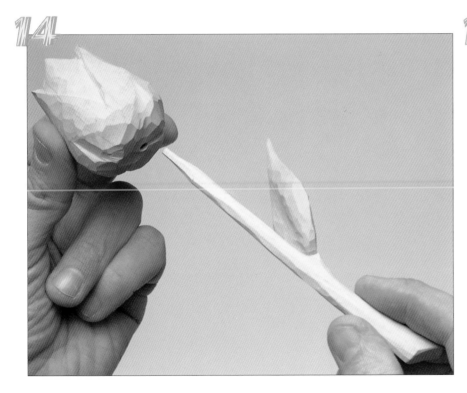

14 For safety, place the flower head in a vice and drill the base to take the stem. You need to choose the right size drill bit for the end of the stem you have carved. You can now assemble your flower by adding a small dab of glue to the leaf and the stem as required.

15 Paint or varnish to complete.

FLOWER IN BLOOM

This is a version of an open flower, similar to the approach described in "Flower in Bud".

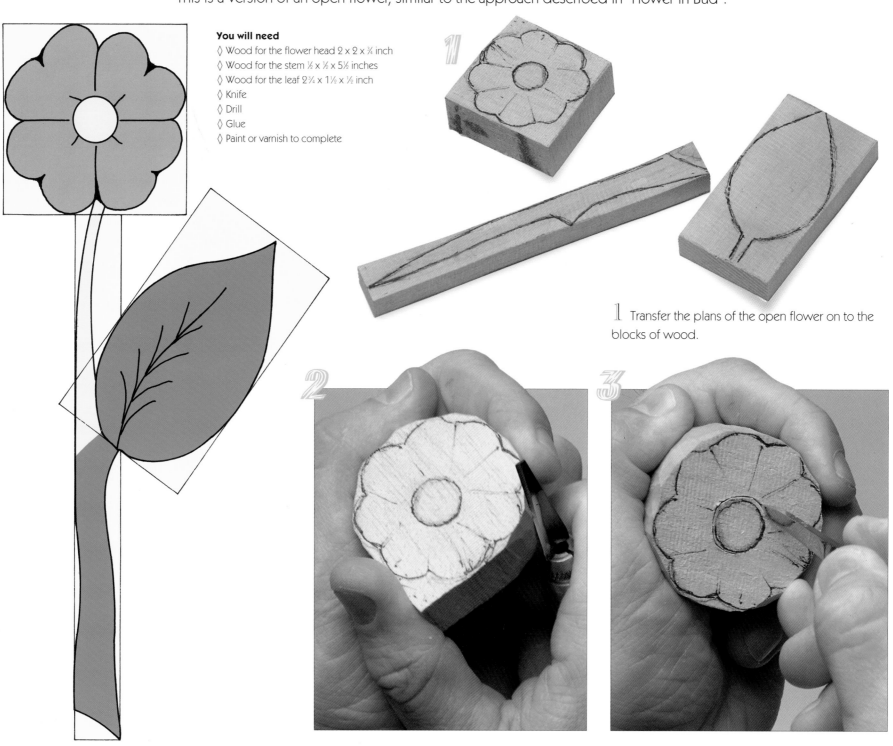

You will need

◊ Wood for the flower head 2 x 2 x ¾ inch
◊ Wood for the stem ½ x ½ x 5½ inches
◊ Wood for the leaf 2¼ x 1½ x ½ inch
◊ Knife
◊ Drill
◊ Glue
◊ Paint or varnish to complete

1 Transfer the plans of the open flower on to the blocks of wood.

2 Start by rounding off the shape of the flower.

3 Mark the center of the flower with your pencil and score around the line.

4 Remove the timber from around the center piece of the flower.

5 Re-mark the petals on the wood.

6 Score along the lines which mark the petals and slightly open the cut with the point of your knife.

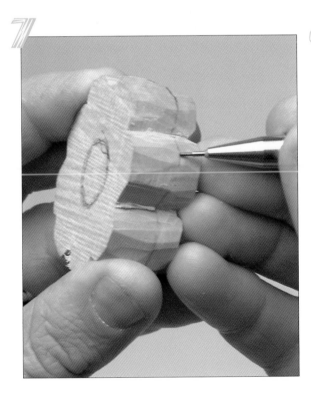

7 Take your pencil and mark a line along the edge of the flower approximately ¼ inch from the face.

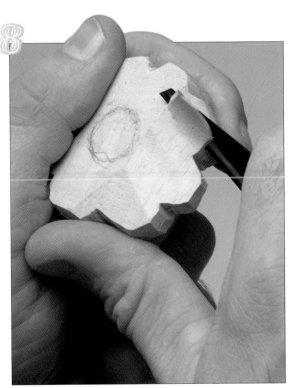

8 Roughly mark the center piece of the flower on the back and carve up to this feature creating a shape roughly like a hat.

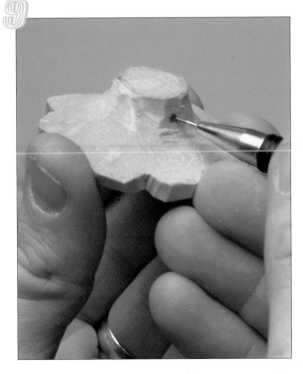

9 This feature is used to locate the stem into the flower head so you need to mark the wood accordingly.

10 Use your plans to create a leaf similar to the previous project but add a line down the center and out from the center to create a little more interest. Follow steps in the previous project to complete.

OWL

Sculptures of owls are very collectable items appearing in all shapes, sizes, and colors. The main feature of this carving is to create the eyes which when looking sideways result in a very attractive little creature.

You will need
◊ Block of wood 2 x 3¼ x 1½ inches
◊ Knife
◊ Paint or varnish to finish

 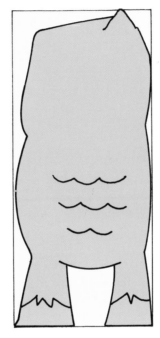 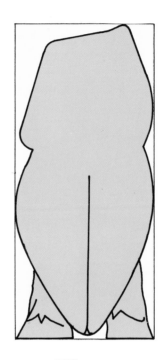

1 Draw the outline of the owl on to your block of wood. Start by carving in the shape of the ears on the top of the head.

2 Carve away the wood from between the back of the feet and the front of the tail. A couple of saw cuts may assist with this.

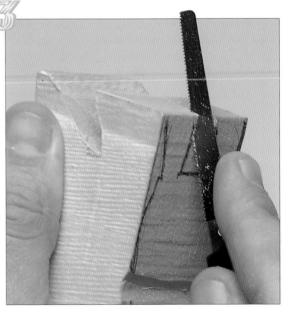

3 Now, take the wood away from between the feet from the front view. Again, a saw cut may assist with this.

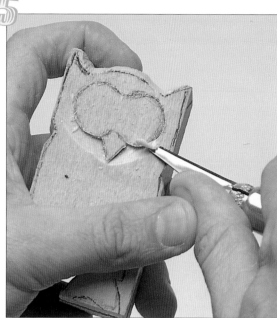

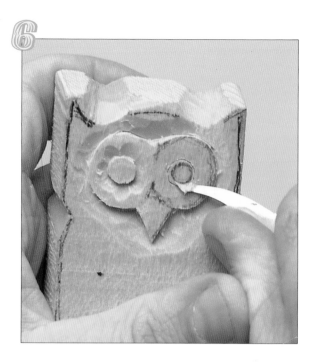

4 Carve away between the legs until you have a nice sweep from the chest down to the tail.

5 Mark the outline of the eyes and beak with your pencil, score along the lines with the tip of your knife and remove the wood from around the cuts.

6 Look at your plan and mark the eye itself in the center of the circle already created. Score along these lines and again remove the wood from the outside.

7 Shape the ears toward the back of the head. Shape the top of the head toward the front to follow the outline of the eyes.

8 Make sure the legs are marked on the block and carve around these to create the front profile.

9 Work a little more on the legs creating some feathering above the feet.

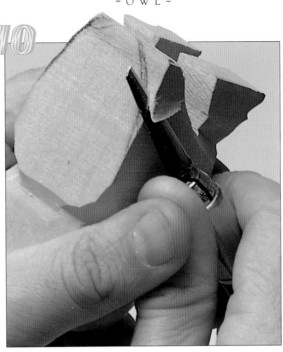

10 Turn to the back of the owl and create the shape indicated in the rear view plan.

11 Refer to your plan and draw in the feathers on the side of the wings.

12 Score in these lines with the tip of your knife and remove wood from just below these cuts.

13 Complete the carving by marking in the pupils of the eyes to make your owl look sideways.

14 Varnish or paint to finish.

BOOT

The boot is a popular and attractive item to carve. It can be used purely as an ornament, or,
if you carve low enough into the ankle it can be used as a container for small dried flowers or
to hold those little items, such as tacks or pins, which you can never find when you want them.

You will need
◊ Block of wood 3¾ x 2 x 1½ inches
◊ Knife
◊ Drill (optional)
◊ Brown wax boot polish

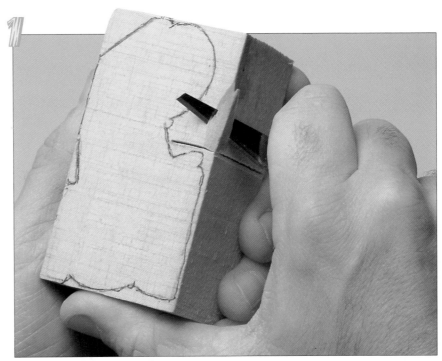

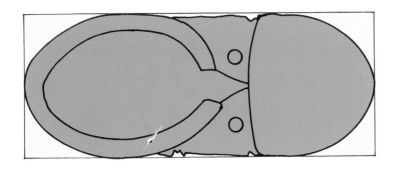

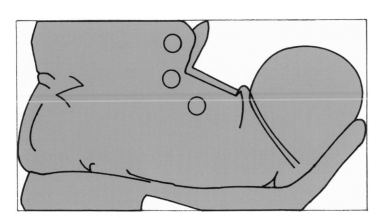

1 Transfer the plan to the block of wood and start carving over the top of the toecap. A saw cut down the front of the ankle part may help.

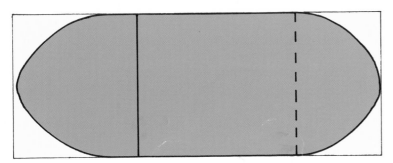

2 Continue by shaping over the toe.

3 Compare your side plan with the carving to complete the work required here.

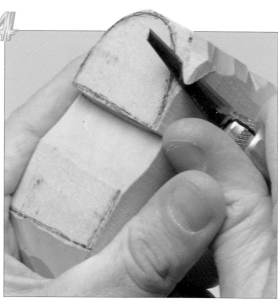

4 Mark the bottom view and carve the shape you require.

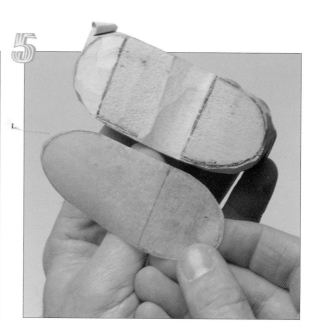

5 Compare your progress with the plan.

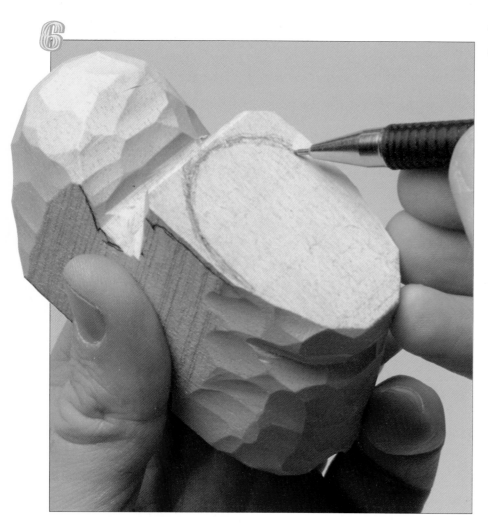

6 Turn now to the ankle and use the top view plan to mark the shape on the block.

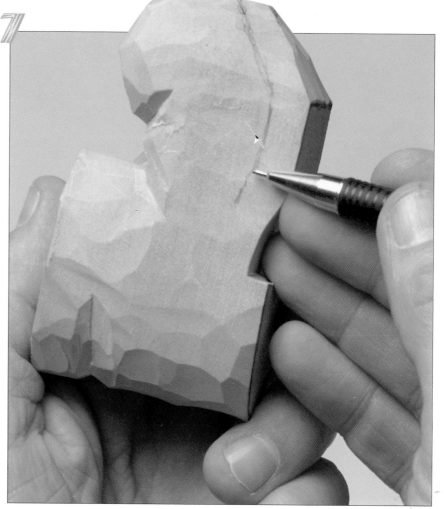

7 Having completed the shape of the ankle mark the sole all around the bottom of the boot.

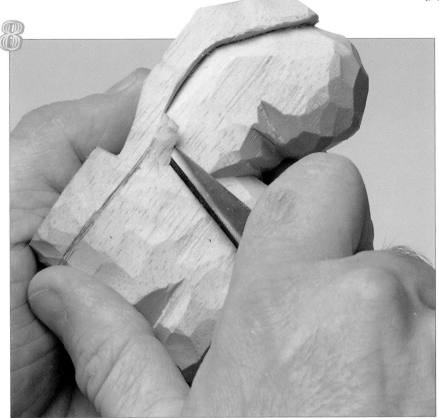

8 Score the line of the sole with the tip of your knife, then remove the wood from above the scored line.

9 Mark on your carving the front of the ankle where the leather separates. In addition mark the thickness of the leather on the ankle.

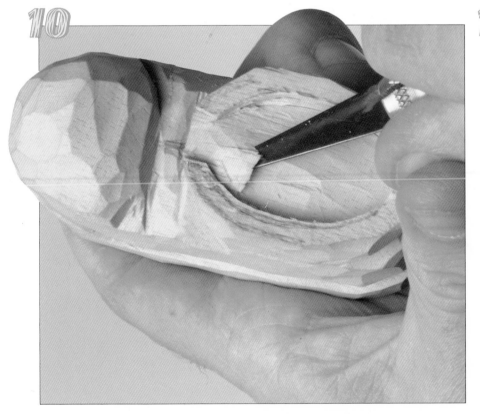

10 Score these lines and remove as much wood from inside the boot as possible.

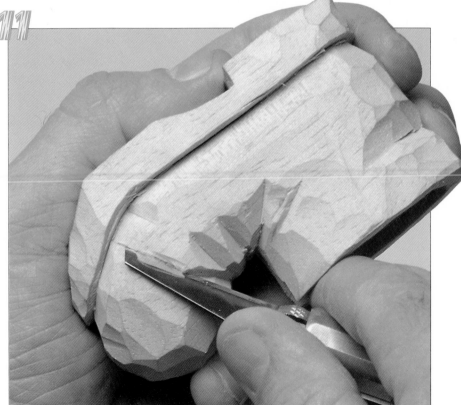

11 Cut in some crease marks over the boot by referring to your plan and carve in the toecap.

12 Mark in the lace holes from the plan and either drill or carve out with the tip of your knife.

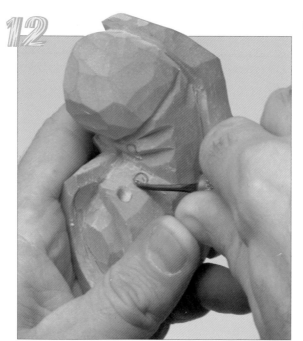

13 An unusual but rather appropriate finish for the boot is to brush with brown wax boot polish which will darken the wood and also create a nice sheen.

CLOWN'S HEAD

Carving faces is a demanding but very rewarding exercise. Faces and figures hold a fascination for most people and if they are done effectively can result in very attractive items. However, much practice is required to develop your skills. The clown's features have been simplified to help you complete this character. You can have fun with your paints in the final stages.

You will need
◊ Block of wood 3 x 2 x 2 inches
◊ Knife
◊ Paint or varnish to finish

1 Transfer the outline from the plan to your block of wood. Mark the outline of the hat from the top and start shaping the block from the bottom of the hairline to the brim.

2 Score along the line which forms the top of the brim and start carving wood away toward the crown of the hat. Cutting directly across the grain will require care and patience.

3 Having formed the top of the brim, shape the crown of the hat.

4 Take your plan and re-mark the outline of the front view onto the wood as well as the lower line of the brim. Score around the line of the brim and shape the hair up to the hat around the whole of the head, repeating the process until you reach the required depth.

5 Carve the shoulders up to the lower hairline around the back and sides.

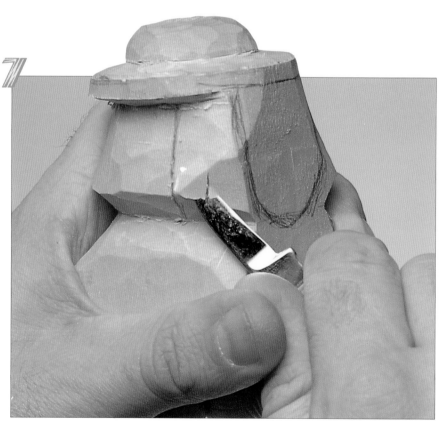

6 Refer to the plan and mark in the front view of the face. In addition mark in the hairline on either side of the head.

7 Score the outline of the hair and remove wood up to the outline of the face on either side.

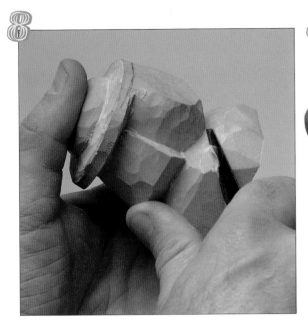

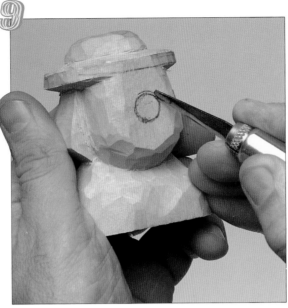

8 Shape the chest and shoulders into the hairline and chin by referring to the plan.

9 The basic shape of the head should now be formed. Referring to the plan mark in the nose and score around this feature with the tip of your knife.

10 Remove wood from around the nose, repeating the scoring to achieve the right depth. You may have to go through this process several times as there is quite a bit of wood to remove. Take care not to damage the brim of the hat.

11 Now, take your pencil and draw in the exaggerated mouth and eyes as shown on the plan.

12 Score over the lines you have drawn and slightly widen these lines with the tip of your knife. Try and raise the mouth by carefully carving the wood from around your cuts. Try and put a little shape into the eyeball and some laughter lines in the corner of the eyes.

13 Mark in the details on the shirt and carve around the scored lines.

14 Complete by varnishing or painting.

CLOWN FULL FIGURE

This project enables you to take what you have learnt in the previous project and carve a full figure. The body has been simplified by placing the hands in the pockets and keeping the stance fairly simple. The overall result is a very appealing character.

You will need
◊ Piece of wood 2 x 2 x 7 inches
◊ Knife
◊ Paint or varnish to finish

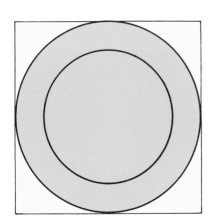

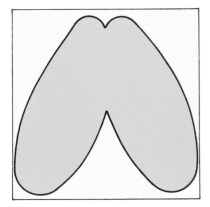

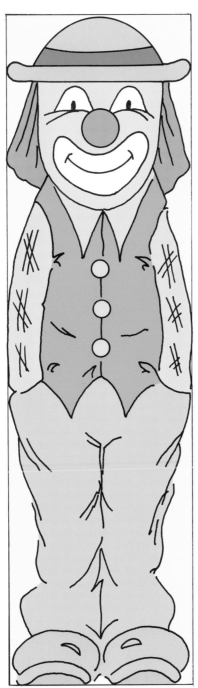

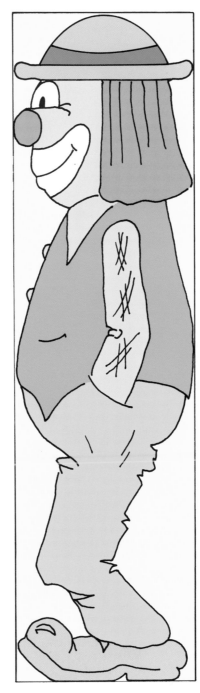

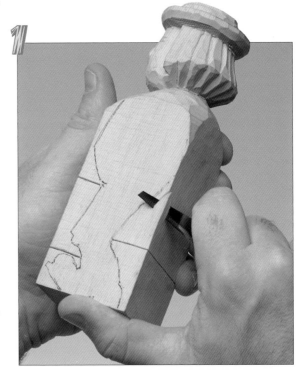

1 Transfer the outlines to your block of wood. Refer to the previous project for details of how to carve the head and shoulders. Start on the body by putting some saw cuts diagonally into the block as shown.

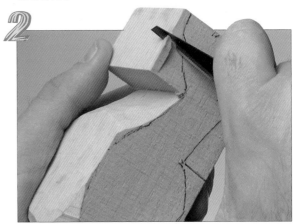

2 Carve in to the saw cuts using the lines transferred from your plans as a guide.

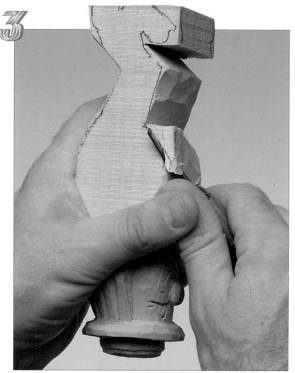

3 Continue this process around all parts of the body.

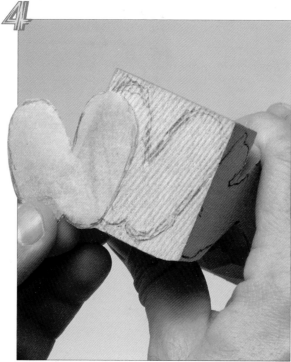

4 Use the plans to mark the feet on the base of the carving.

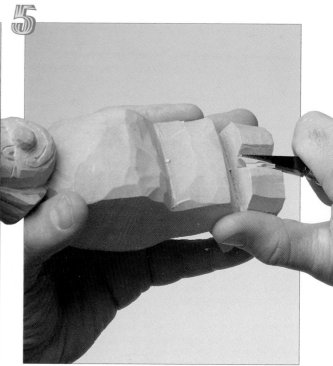

5 Shape the feet referring to the base as required.

6 Use your side view plan to locate the arms on either side.

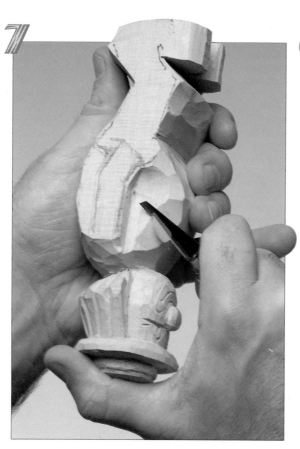

7 Score in the arms and the pockets and carve away the wood from in front of the arm.

8 Repeat the process behind the arm and then on the other side of the body.

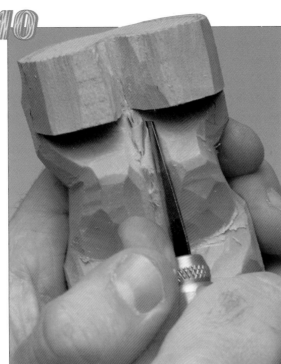

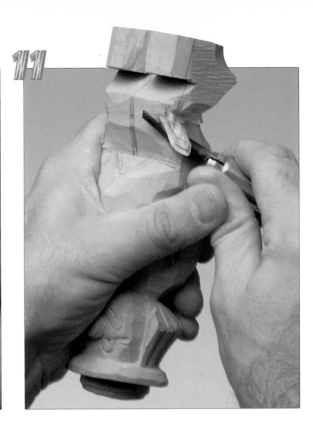

9 Use your front view plan to check how deep you should cut the arms.

10 Return to the legs and separate each leg in line with the feet.

11 Start shaping the legs trying to get a baggy effect in the trousers.

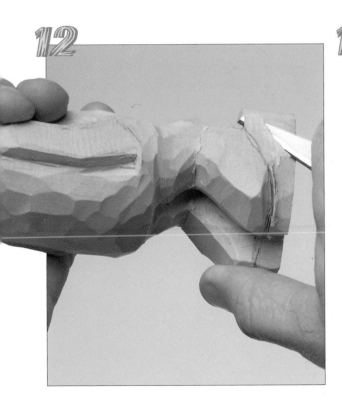

12 Mark in the bottom of the trousers. Score the line and carve wood away from below to form the feet. Refer to your plans to put more shape into the feet.

13 Mark in the soles of the shoes, score the line and remove wood from above the line and further shape the shoe. You can refer to the Boot project for more detail on this part of the carving.

14 Once you are happy with the general shape of the body, start marking in the detail i.e. waistcoat, collar, buttons, crease marks, etc. Score all these lines and carve away from the outside to complete.

15 Varnish or paint to complete.

START-A-CRAFT